CONFER

Ahren Warner was born in 1986, and grew up in Lincolnshire before moving to London. He received an Eric Gregory Award in 2010 and is completing a PhD in philosophy and literature at the University of London. He has published his work widely in magazines and anthologies, including *Identity Parade* (2010) and *Voice Recognition* (2009) from Bloodaxe, and in *Re:*, a pamphlet from Donut Press. His first book-length collection, *Confer* (Bloodaxe Books, 2011), is a Poetry Book Society Recommendation. He divides his time between Paris and London.

AHREN WARNER
CONFER

BLOODAXE BOOKS

ISBN: 978 1 85224 914 4

First published 2011 by
Bloodaxe Books Ltd,
Highgreen,
Tarset,
Northumberland NE48 1RP.

www.bloodaxebooks.com
For further information about Bloodaxe titles
please visit our website or write to
the above address for a catalogue.

Supported by
**ARTS COUNCIL
ENGLAND**

Cover design: Neil Astley & Pamela Robertson-Pearce.

Printed in Great Britain by
Bell & Bain Limited, Glasgow, Scotland.

For Joe Warner

ACKNOWLEDGEMENTS

Acknowledgements are due to the editors of the following publications in which some of these poems have previously appeared: *Best British Poetry 2011* (Salt Publishing, 2011), *City State: New London Poetry* (Penned in the Margins, 2009), *Identity Parade: New British and Irish Poetry* (Bloodaxe Books, 2010), *Magma*, *Pen Pusher*, *Poetry London*, *Poetry Review*, *Pomegranate*, *The White Review*, *The Wolf* and *Voice Recognition: 21 Poets for the 21st Century* (Bloodaxe Books, 2009). A selection of these poems have appeared previously as a pamphlet, *Re:* (Donut Press, 2010). I would like to acknowledge the support of Arts Council England for an award I received from them in 2008 as well the Society of Authors for the Eric Gregory Award I received in 2010.

I would especially like to thank Roddy Lumsden for his years of help, support and editorial advice. I would like to thank Andy Ching, Patrick Brandon, Andrew Jamison, Matthew Caley, Imogen Robertson, A.B. Jackson, Heather Phillipson, and Joe and Jan Warner, all of whom have contributed to this book in many and various ways. Finally I would like to thank Elle for all her love and support.

CONTENTS

CONFER

I

To love is to give what you haven't got.

JACQUES LACAN, Le Séminaire X 'L'angoisse'

La rue assourdissante autour de moi hurlait.
Longue, mince, en grand deuil, douleur majestueuse,
Une femme passa, d'une main fastueuse
Soulevant, balançant le feston et l'ourlet;

CHARLES BAUDELAIRE, À une passante

Jardin du Luxembourg

Here, all parks are masculine, grammatically so
I mean: *le jardin*, *le parc*, never a *la*.
Planes defined by avenues, circulars,
lines on the maps labelled with saints, saintly
politicos: Saint Michel, Kennedy, Jacques.

Even the flowers, here, are masculine;
reminding us of the season, a year or so back,
Gucci, or some such, had men preening
in powder-pink shirts, strutting their cocks
down the Strand, Bishopsgate, Bank.

Here, there are no pink shirts, hardly any
shirts at all. Just men, reclining in the bronze
of their *estomacs*; the vague swell of their guts
rising to the heat. There are women too, of course,
mostly with tops, but tops rolled up,

estomacs bared to the sun. We are reclining too,
squinting at the sky – as electric, if lighter
than Klein's – swallowed up or slipping in
to an igloo of *sérénité*, the gender of which
I've had neither the time, nor desire, to look up.

La brisure

each toll sustains itself   as if expecting
its own next sounding   or   another's

to which it will defer   by default   falling
to its own lack   its spacing from the other

each space comes   tactile   as a relief
or   as the rough joint-lines of a bronze

the repetition   of a hollowed   motif
the becoming sound   of the bronze

so each bell seems   to long
for an end   less partition   than party

a silence on which   each sound   hangs
for its self-sameness   its being *partie*

you listen   to the last toll   draining
retained only   in the space   it becomes

you're unsure   if you're still waiting
or hearing   what has come

Hasard

Think *Taraxacum officinale* – a dandelion clock –
just that, and not
the idyll;
the product of focus groups, sanitised ads.

Please, forget the infants, their still-taut mothers,
the hyper-green grass.
And, if you can't
abstract a singular, globular head of seeds

– a greyish, Baudelairean candyfloss –
make the background
a patchy scrubland
or better still, a fissure of concrete.

And so... And so a halitosis wind kicks up
and sets off
each germ
upon its path. You lack the intellect, so

let's call such combinatorics
chance.
And let's
forget Coriolis, the geostrophic balance;

let us recall only the *lits hasardeux*
– those beds of chance –
in which
we have landed, taken root, read

'hazard, from *al-zahr* (the die), or
yasara (he played at dice)'.

Brumes et pluies

after Baudelaire

To the ends of autumn, winter, spring
– mud-drenched and soporific –
I love you and offer up this hymn,
as you envelop *kardia* and *cortex*
in a gauzy cerement of mist.

The wind brawls and nips
at the moor's expanse;
the weathercock is rusted hoarse;
the nights are long and nothing

is sweeter to a gloom-congested heart
on which the dew has formed and frozen
than you – livid seasons, pale shadows.

Unless, of course, it's a moonless night,
an accidental bed; that lull of suffering.

About suffering they were never wrong, The Old Masters...

Though, when it comes to breasts, it's a different story.
Cranach, for example, never seems to have progressed
beyond his pubescent attempts at apprenticeship:

tennis balls sewn to a pillow of hay, fingers coming
to terms with the concept of foreplay. So too
with Titian, whose *Venus* bares handleless plungers

or the fruits of a template mocked up at Bellini's.
For breasts, you want Rochegrosse, his *Chevalier*
surrounded by breasts real enough to have men

gripping their gallery plans discreetly; or Picabia
at his most garish: his naked, peroxidised blonde
stretching to coddle her slavering mutt. Her breasts

impress their tender weight upon us, and though
not as lofty as Pieter would have liked, she too
knows something of our weakness; that we fall

and are floored as much by the salt lure of skin.

Suite de danses
(for Elle)

I

Often, once or twice a day, often
more – with a slight shudder –

I conjure, involuntary, an image
of my death. More, perhaps,

a scenario: most often cancer,
as often it's my heart

giving. Sometimes something more
obscure: choking on Mozzarella.

Just now, out on the hot roof,
it was falling through and onto,

into fire. And yes, it made me think –
annoyingly, I know – of Arnaut:

Sovenha vos a temps de ma dolor...

II

I have an obsessional's tick
that has me tapping at my head

each time I think like this
(half to wager good luck,

half to bat such thoughts
away). Today, though, I try

to 'remember', to *Sovenha*,
Arnaut's 'suffering', which means

trying to think the pinch of fire,
pangs ripening to molten pain.

And though I can think, I think,
how he must have screamed

as those first flames nipped,
somewhere, between bubble

and peel, I come up short;
unable or unwilling to think

absolute pain, self-immolation,
the awful ecstasy of passion.

III

Rather, it's you – my darling – weeping
I'm thinking of. It's your lips' soft broil.

It's that I'd rather burn than fail
to comfort you with this: our long

remorseless clinch, our beatific fusion.

Dactylogram (Nietzsche)

Skipping the 'tache, moving straight to the fact
or spurious rumour that,
one night, you strolled
through Basel, or Naumberg, intent on a harlot

and that not any old slut would do,
but only the crustiest madam;
so bow-legged
and furrowed, you were assured of the clap.

I remembered this – your syphilitic tryst,
your will to tragedy, your wish
for an end spent bathing
in your own glossolalia and shit –

at the bar of a Nuremberg brothel
we'd mistaken
for a kitsch euro-club
and blabbed your gossip on our hurried retreat

through settling snow, unknown *Straßen*.

Dactylogram (Nietzsche)

I remembered you too, in a derelict camp
turned museum, a hundred clicks south

of that Nuremberg square, its bronze
Meister Wagner. The snow was still thick

and embossed with 'Happy Christmas'
stamped out in child-sized footprints.

I remembered you, amongst the battery
of beds and the *Dusche*; the bronzed

ovens lined up in the next room.
Somewhere, between pockmarked *Stämme*,

I muttered your catchphrase: *Gott ist todt.*
Gott bleibt todt. Und wir haben ihn getödtet.

Rosenmontag

In Munich   the trams still run   though snow hunkers
beside the tracks   and each building looks beyond

repair   baying to buckle   onto the *platz*.
There   we are all   varying degrees of drunk

on steins of beer   or cartons   of sweet wine
shared in swigs.   Sarah bemoans a groper.

Locals hunker to a doorstep   one pulls a girl
towards him.   She dribbles sweet   *Ich liebe Dich*

and means it.   I mean   she's not just cooing
through that mist   of exhaled booze   and snow

sublimándum   under a crowd's foot.   I can't set
meaning to her words   but feel it   how she intones

herself to him   presses each sound   as a tender fact
that will not be solicited.   Sarah is pressed against me.

Legare

This   is what I consign   perhaps   because my hands fall cold
on the eys of a harpsichord   or my right arm fails to bow
a sustained   viola note.   Or   because I do not wear
breeches at the court   of some Germanic state

do not listen   to the latest offering   of a Herr Mozart
eyeing the women   the aristocrats   those in waiting
or catch their eyes   proceed to bed them
the scandal of high societies: Dresden   Vienna   Venice.

Because   I do not mark this world   with pale cottons
and the hues of birthing girls   bastards   who'll grow
to their own actions   and sadness   coaxing warm tears
from other's eyes   blurred   before books whose words

blot and run   so nothing is known
but affect   and afflicted men   holding or held by
women in straw beds;   spare light
from candles near done;   the kestrel   lingering   outside.

La Gare

The *train* is *en retard*   there has been a *perturbation*.
I am perturbed that my mean   interior   little child

won't drop it   that he finds so very *amusant*
this homonym;   that he grins his nasty little smile

at the LEDs that sign *'retard'*.   The sophists say
a lot   and some of it   is right on the money:

that we'd have been better off   not born   say
or that man was born too late.   Lately

the métro has often been delayed.   My terrible
inner bastard transmogrifies   has become

each of us   – Iapetus' sons –   scrunching up his little
encephalopathic face.   The train finally comes.

A bustle of Pierres and Sabines   and I'm on...
and home to my love   to my *kalon kakon*.

Pictogramme

O, you – a hundred years from now – do you remember
the TV? It was shite really, a feckless invention;

nowhere near as useful as your gamma-ray
carving knives, which both cook and cut together.

Either way, it was on TV that I heard
Senhora Rego declared 'the greatest living painter

of woman's experience' by this bloke from Australia
(do you still have Australia, or have you

abolished it?). And, perhaps this is a moot point
for you, my highly evolved future readers,

but I wondered how he knew. I mean, how he
could know the *adequatio* of colour, line and texture

to the experience of something so utterly Other.
Here I'm speaking to you, future males; females

transpose the gender. On Avenue de l'Opéra
or Rue des Petits Champs, I find myself so often

fixated by a girl's *derrière*, trying to think over
the rubbing of two thighs; nothing between but air.

Re:

As soup made Eliot think of Spinoza
and *she* made Donne think of compasses,
drummers drumming bring to mind ἀλήθεια

and how, for the Greeks, truth was uncoveredness;
drummers true drummers only by their drumming,
tangled thighs the criterion of lovers.

And my point, true love, is that I've been thinking
and don't think I can love someone who struggles
with the latent – flowers well before blooming –

whose gifts must, without fail, be spectacles
and never a package of crêpe paper and dirt
which, water added, might turn to vegetables:

artichokes, small but incontrovertibly *vert*;
the promise of a purple patch next year.

Sonetto

You want to feel   your lungs stutter
the diaphragm's stammer;   that tear

snug in its duct   to fall
to feel yourself give   to a sadness

beyond or before   language.

Outside   shutters   *balcons*
Haussman's façades   the odd

growl of a car   gliding along
slipping between   the city's slick

the scent and silence   of its sleep.

More than anything   you want
to pad your way across   the hall;

to slip between the covers;   to feel
the surety   transmitted in her warmth.

Confer

The varieties of household paint proliferate;
Crown's glosses, matts and silks spill over,
fill the book I find between Catullus

and Celan. Donaghy and Donne
flank a Dulux brochure. And yes
I'm trying to show how well-read I am,

or trying a line between compulsion
and abandon – the just-off alphabetical
I've whittled to a totem – a prop

with which to strut the bounds
of personality. *Contradiction in coherence
expresses the force of desire*, apparently.

Elysium

As, at Alesia, Gaieus licked
the Gauls,
Mackerel would fillet Beckett
with his *canif*.

And, as Vercingétorix
was laid low,
at Alesia Beckett slumps
near the Métro.

Above, Radnitzky shoots
a young Artaud,
Tichenor, Messrs Joyce
and Cocteau

while Beckett hangs in there
by a *filum*,
slouched and spilling claret,
barely *vif*

but lives, of course, to earn
his laurels
unlike Vercingétorix who,
rubbing his galls,

dawdles among the asphodels,
eyeing the next field on.

Métro

Take a second for a double take –
not at this crowd
heaving,
but at *that* blonde, her breasts on show

and, if you can, scrape your eyes up
to the line of her nose;
how it seeps
into cheeks, how they're rouged high.

It's not that I want you to see
how special she is,
she's not.
Rather, I want you to notice

how her line and seep is a certain kind;
a certain combo
of nose and cheek;
how her face is one of *those* faces

and how, if I'd singled out any other
girl or guy, you'd see the same:
a kind
of face, a scion of our bough –

this growth of soft flesh, rattling minds,
just asking to be cut down.

Beach

Inside   you let the spray   course through your hair;
the water rolls down your back   narrows its path

through the nook of your spine   falls at   and around
your toes.   The sea-breeze is cold.

His words contract   the interior conglomerate
of muscles   men of faith   might call the soul.

He ambulates fear so delicately   those human tones
of despair.   I do not know   if the spray of salt

buffeting my lips   is the cold.   I snag
my breath on the air   the depth of misery

he conjures   in a few uncommon words   though
we see it every day: a jaw tensed like a scaffold

the twitch of skin   ill at ease on its frame   smiles
that seem pleas.   I slow lick

the sea from my lips   and turn to our room.
I want to lick   the water that beads to your skin;

the soft relief   of something that fits.

Harmonie du soir
(after Baudelaire)

Each shaking, dewy sod
expels scent like a censer.

The ground's sweat
turns the dawn air.

The still pumping bass,
the lingering treble

expels scent like a censer.

Each speaker shakes
an afflicted heart.

The still pumping bass,
the lingering treble,

the sky an altar –
beautiful, orphic.

Each speaker shakes
an afflicted heart.

Tender, hating
the amaranthine cavern,

the sky is an altar:
beautiful, orphic.

The sun jitters
through its grume,

tender, hating
the amaranthine cavern.

We clutch scraps
of our phosphor-lit past,

the sun jitters
through its grume;

memory is luminescent
like a scar.

I *La Carte Postale*

As we say arboretum   here   I walk below the *arbres*
down the Rue Jussieu   amongst the mottled *ombre*.

The books shrink on their stalls   the shop walls crack
to craquelure.   The Seine might be the Acheron

if   Eliot had got his *langue* on.   The cafés brim.
The heat ensures an ambery slick   above the upper lip

part pimento   tar   and garlic   but miscible
with the Beaujolais   I'm drinking   by the bottle.

From bed   I hear Emmanuel   the bourdon
bell   (at Notre Dame   the tourists shout him down).

Outside   the traffic drones   a Pérotin melisma.
As always   I think of you   I wish that you were here.

II *Tempo di Menuetto*

The books shrink on their stalls, the shop walls crack,
panes begin to stutter,

the pigeons take their leave, foundations shudder,
shuck their own six feet of earth.

The rubble forms – a rough cartography of our fall –
dust flukes upon the air.

Here, I hold your tongue, its ferric tang, the way
it sets the moon beyond the body.

III Works and Days

As rubble forms   its rough cartography of our fall
but tells little or nothing   of much but beauty.

As such rubble is nothing   but symptoms or sultry
reminders we're flesh   that we ache above all.

As we have little   but the sultry gestures of lovers;
our outlines pressed   into patches of grass.

As the little we have   must be shared with others
or rationed   or sterilised by the glass.

As Hesiod said   to the girls from Pieria
we're haply destined   to love our destruction.

As faith is the condition   by which we sin
so I think of you   I wish you were here.

II

Morta fra l'onde è la ragion e l'arte,

PETRARCH, Canzoniere 189

What is the language using us for?
It uses us all and in its dark
Of dark actions selections differ.

W.S. GRAHAM, 'What Is The Language Using Us For?'

Léman

Here, at the river's kink, southbank and north
are lost to a city slanting towards
some hinter point
where fabled chimneys meet fabled hills.

Here – where sink estates and conurbations
are forgotten
for the cumulus,
the glare of windows, the plated dome,

light cumulative, the air an illuminated cold –
you watch the scurry,
trying to divine
the salt glimmer behind each eye;

a scar set as crystalline, and reading:
unhappy child,
languid marriage,
frayed knot of poverty and desire.

Homage to E3

...a retinal twitch.   And the day still   black ink bled grey
the excess running to clot in the gutter   with socks   render

from patchy shops   a silt screed   over pavement slabs
sifted   from foot to foot   passed between strangers.

The *light* though   has turned   from *plucked*   to reed
glissando;   an irreal shift   from seen to wadding.

You   in your jeans   that leave your legs flagpoles
your face *sous rature*   hacked cough   have been romantic.

The sun is going down   through bare trees and behind
tower-blocks   windows turned phosphor   smog-orange

with softened light   skulked back   through stairwells
remaindered   through west-facing windows   to grace east

finding us shifting   foot to foot   on a street corner
the air a definite   pizzicato.   Here   my breath

is the first glut   since a child   stuttering into the garden
ruddy faced   lungs singing   clear with oxygen.

Near St Mary Woolnoth

I doubt even your authenticity – tree
amongst this boom of tinted glass, landscaped grass
and men whose Windsor-knotted ties shout *phallus*.

We both know these streets feel best long after
the faded linger of a caretaker's patter,
the guard's breath as loud as his lull will allow;

that this city is felt in a drunken swagger,
the hop of a barrier, ascents via shimmy
and shin that find you high on a balcony.

Teeter, titter through beer, mutter the view
of the river, windows turned baubles, the buzz
of a night-time generator. Shout *bow low*

multitudes. Know that the city has nothing
to offer but loopholes, itself as a playground
adventure, that to find yourself stumped

at the foot of a tree, suspicious of its age,
that its bark's wizened nature was planned,
is to miss the point entirely.

The Carpenters Arms

Heroclitus implies the clitoris sits close enough to witness
the crux of metaphysics;
a stream in which the fetishist can bathe but once.

Unlike, of course, Cratylus, slurping his Bud and babbling
about *a stream impossible to bathe in.*
Either way, Lacan insists, *man does not come... to enjoy*

a woman's body... but enjoys the organ. Which, as he's aware,
irritates Parmenides, who slurs that
according to men's opinions, things come into being.

Meaning, I guess, that having it off is having it off, or
it's the same thing
that can be thought and that can be. Descartes agrees.

The hot, blonde barmaid stoops an inch to serve
five pints, pickled eggs,
the *finitised infinite*, the gape of her low-cut shirt.

Aristotle is a C___

I'm in love with detail. Chestnut trees
SEAN O'BRIEN, 'Walking'

Not the vagaries   of sprawled   variegated leaves
or the monotony   of rows of tree after tree
but this canyoned ridged knot   half dying wood   half moss

that   makes its cranny at the foot   of a burnt-out stump
and if sketched   would be feigned   with approximate lines
by an eye   unqualified to deal in minutiae.

Yet   such detail is here: the cragged bark   petrol seared
the odd ribbed louse   the intestinal villi of moss
the etched insignia   *kezza n nosh woz ere.*

This last one is our *ex machina*   a middle finger
to black lines on white pages   to the sanitised sign.
Bow down   to this make-shift god   of pen-knife and passion

like kezza   at nosh's request   moving to genuflect.

Hangin' Round

Schooled by proxy via Freiburg and Ulm
and knowing,
as far as possible, that
'to risk meaning nothing is to start', I have

an aversion – the kind an old Etonian has
to untucking his shirt –
to *truth*,
let alone eternal truths, let alone

eternal truths recalled through the words
of a musician,
let alone
eternal truths recalled through the words

of a musician I've heard, on more than one occasion,
described as a *poet*.
Still,
'you're still doing things I gave up years ago'

are the words that come to mind, here
in this Middle England city
barely
big enough to be a town, with its small-town feel;

its Starbucks worn like a medal
of cosmopolitan rank;
its battered,
mock Louisiana-style 'deli'

where, incidentally, I remember sipping coffee
with a girl who loved 'drinking coffee'
more than coffee
half a decade ago, and who, as I recall,

'hated the immigrants', but smelt of truffles
and ambergris
and who, so I've heard,
spends her time, these days, on the rush-hour train
to a smaller small town, where she's training to be
an accountant...

Grimsby

An old dock town
where the last sailor is long drowned
and the boats rot, creaking

like gravel-throated cancer patients
singing canticles, croaking
polyp-splintered, khoomei paeans.

Carolina

(After Frank Zappa, George Gershwin, The Raconteurs, Counting Crows, Claudia Church, Alabama, Bucky Covington, Sheryl Crow, Brand New, Mary Black, James Taylor, Jo Dee Messina and Josh Turner)

Having always thought, someday, I'd burn that bed,
I left with nothing but a cold bologna sandwich,
a borrowed suit, pockets full of dust and found myself

a thousand miles away, amongst the mountain dew
and, later, amongst smokey mountain eyes
in a crowded back-room, where every look was thrown

like a knife and I thought the game was over, but
sitting on three queens I made a train at sunrise.
That night, I swallowed liquor and a lighter

and found her like moonlight falling on a bed.
I could have swore her hair was made of rayon
and when we kissed she tasted like a loaded gun.

The sound of bluegrass and southern words
wove their ways to an old Sandlapper tune
between Palmetto trees and geese in flight.

Wearing a Milton-Bradley crayon, she whispered
something warm about the height of cotton,
asked if I could feel the moon shine

and beneath the silver sun I asked her
what she'd say to setting out for getting lost.
She sent me to the milkman, looking for the truth.

Sonetto

So   there's some charm in this   us waking up
with breath   a cross   between dog and sewer
my queasy sentence   already begun
and yours still lurking   around the corner.

My infatuation is   your unmade face
still sweet through sleep   and the slick of beer.
It cites the curve of your cheek   the freckles
of your nose   your pillow-smudged mascara.

And let's not pretend: last night my eyes veered
to the plunge   of that   girl's jumper
where wool-mix met   peach-skin breasts
and my pheromones   stamped out a samba.

Still   in this fresh hour   I lap your scent
and know   such glances are   but simulacra.

Opus

That note, in Buckley's rendition
of Cohen, should exist

as the only definition for 'fucked'
– as in 'I'm fucked'.

There is a point, somewhere,
around twenty seconds in

to a Seattle-birthed song
that embodies the word 'abandon'.

So too with the dab of his foot
to the Whirlwind Selector turning

acoustic to distortion;
the sublating of silence that occurs

in that bar of the Allegro
of that Bruch Konzertstück.

There was a girl at school who'd say
I'd end up a rock star or in prison.

I'm neither, have nothing,
but an art I've been learning

too long; a subject
I've studied beyond flogged.

Base

Aren't our stock phrases funny   how they tip off the tongue
having lain there   (*like a lion   the thing is   rough as a cob*)
they nuzzle in our throats so our first re-pliant breath   births

old utterances   to snugly fit   new situations   or old ones
made distinctly new   by the trick   of light modifications:
a different girl   a strange locale   a taste you can't quite tell

though you know some of it is cumin   and some   a herb
that could only be one of two   verisimilar
either of which   would add a twist to our stock stock

of water   leeks   onions and bay leaves   halved carrots
sharp showers and trains   estates   and white-washed suburbia
held hands and TV shows   photographs and miscellanea

souped-up   with the sound   of hailstone on granite
sweat-fused bodies   lemon juice   cayenne pepper.

Engram

As the wrinkled skin of milk over-boiled
conjures the sludge of moistening bath balls,

the pucker of wet paper – graphite's aquaplane –
summons up bubble bath, its faux-clementine.

And, though I know that a single memory
so often beacons through our infant clutter,

I'm surprised that (though only a decade ago)
I remember the red, the nap of the pyjamas

I shed for the bath; how urgent it seemed
to run bare-arsed and dangling

in search of a pen and the paper I'd hold
in muculent hands; each letter bleeding

to a smutch or shadow. I remember this.
I cannot remember my first kiss's name.

Legare

I've learned to love olives and choked on the bitter
tint of coffee till gag turned to gulp. I insist
on perusing the wine sections of supermarkets
reciting your criteria: from age to alcohol by volume.

I've internalised your habits and will reproof
anyone who dares a half-hearted attempt
at the washing of vegetables. That the gas is turned off
is something to be ascertained more than once

comme avec mes clefs ou la lock, which I check
and check again. I'm in the habit of switching
languages to see who will blanch, and
– in Fitzgerald's vein – consider elitism

a cardinal virtue; can't help a creeping distain
in the company of Etonians, where my accent reverts
to a Northernness it never had. At night I repeat
myself stories, till I find the slippage of sleep.

Attesa

Not   the grandiosity of a giant
standing on one side   of the valley

shouting   across to another
giant   standing   on the opposite hill

while   the minions prick up
their ears   invariably   failing to hear.

And not   the altruism   of accepting
one's place   as master   or slave

but the *jouissance*   of making
that one   simple   mark   like

what's-his-name   Fontana
standing alone   and hearing the wind

echoing   his old   school teacher
taking the day's   attendance.

Avis

Give them time to miss you   and if they don't
call   imagine that they want to   somewhere;

that their smile is there   but worn as cant
that whoever they're with   is a Gaussian blur

as are the trees   the red-breasts   the children
playing in the background   as they stare

beyond the scent   brimming in the kitchen
the tender fit   of another's hand

that gaggle of friends   laughing around them.
Think of their eyes   set on a point beyond

the earth's curve   or that stretch of summer
light   they wear like a cosy   burden

waiting   as they must be   for you.   Venture
hope: that they might be happy   even there.

Cuneiform

A scar in the centre of my palm, the perfect fit for one of those nails; the kind they nail loud-mouth folks to crosses with.

On my left thumb, a pale scythe gained one night with a bread knife. Yes – far past drunk – having drunk all night with an eidolon of mine turned mate.

Another, on my right pinkie, a curved squiggle won with an act of melodrama: a fist through a square of glass, a fizzling quadrate.

Should I mention you, K, who often fell in the shower? The times I found you bandaged, swaddling the latest signing to your safestore of scars; kerfs that would turn brain-matter white.

Control, you said, textbook of course. And, as I didn't say: hold tight, try to look for the boy grinning on your next flight, through stutters, spasmodic light, condensation sparking near an engine.

Which is my way of saying no, all mine are incidental; inevitable, if you like.

November

The fireworks burst like others' revelry,
like the cheer of the upstairs flat's party

– those neighbours you never quite met –
dull through floorboards and fibreglass.

The kitten moans outside; raindrops
parachute, flutter down like eyelashes.

No one is there to take them
between finger and thumb and ask you

to close your eyes, to blow your wishes,
to send them skittering into reality.

The fireworks arc above Suburbiton
– launched from a field with a licence –

like a council-approved expression
of rapture. The rain is unchecked

and rouses to a damped staccato.

Διόννσος

Girl with ridiculous earrings   why do you bother
to slap the boy   we all assume is your boyfriend
and is lolling over   that bus seat   shouting

it's a London thing.   He is obviously a knob
but a happy one   and that   it seems to me
is the important   though not localisable   thing.

αἱ μοῦσαι

London Bridge, having seen its trawl of fruit and fish, having felt the patter of countless bluchers,
was taken apart pillar by arch. All this is common knowledge. So too that it was brokered

to a *puke* named MacCulloch, who'd managed to mistake it for another, more iconic, two blocks downriver.
Less known are those New Haven masons, fuelled by new money and nostalgia,

armed with alginate and plaster, who came. And left with casts of Oxford grandeur,
reliefs and rubbings of bas-reliefs, with which to hem their new-build halls, their fledgling culture.

Of course, as they sourced their Old Country theme-parks, we swapped them for Americana.
Traffic is two-way. Here, the traffic's heavy; the bus is stuck in front of a 'hoppin centr'

whose font and façade once said: come in, we're the closest thing you'll get to getting in a Catalina,
a powder-blue tux, to palming wide lapels, to purring down a boulevard in Santa Monica.

In Arizona, tourists tread the dull beige brick. The English Village is falling down.

Μνημοσύνη

The smackhead's hands are soft and clammy
like the just-lathered palms of my mother.
I remember

his pupils are an absolute
torpor, a squall of fear, and have me
as a little boy in the doorway, watching

my mother in the midst of laundry
and tears, and what seemed inconceivable
grief.

It is the give of his skin that lingers
or muscles its way back in, *here*

between that Cranach the Elder crucifixion
and this crucifixion by an elderly Cranach.

Ἐρινύες

Paint fragments captured
like Muybridge or Marey.

Keep the background as simple
as possible, and brilliant.

Between netting and brick
set that point between smiling

and screaming. As in
that portrait of Peter looking

over his shoulder, or
the attitude of apes staring

into a mirror. Think of Rodin,
of a head cupped in hands;

a figure standing on carpet
or lying on sofa; turning, or

making love; crouching, as from
that photograph of a lion.

Paint a landscape of fish
or dogs on the rail. Concentrate.

With corrugated iron, tiles,
upside down nudes

against curtains. Force
a kind of self-portrait. Think

alizarin crimson, windsor green.

Θάνατος

I have read the books   and can mime *fort/da*,
the *chora*   how the mind fires   below language
fits with desire   how it drives us to death.

Yet   I can only speak of longing   how I find it
in these songs   the ones that seem to sweat
adolescent nights: the crackle of soap bar;

thighs coaxed   from her naughty-nurse's dress;
the texture of sick.   Songs that pulse
with the glottal stops of this drink   here

          where the night sings   with its promise
of a mind wiped clean   hushes the prospect
of morning   of waking to nothing.

Whoso list to hunt…

*In "poetical" discourse, the communication
of the existential possibilities of one's state
-of-mind can become an aim in itself…
this amounts to a disclosing of existence.*
                        MARTIN HEIDEGGER, Being and Time

As the hoplites sobbed *Thalatta!* to the sea,
we read of them in Xenophon, or *Ulysses*,

but felt nothing. Or if not nothing, not
that sediment of earth and sweat

giving to tears, growing to rivulets,
which, reaching the lips, would taste

half of the earth, half of the sea. So,
I can't stop thinking of you, Elisabet,

or the arc you make of yourself
beneath the pressure of two palms

around that stretch – between your navel
and your breasts – bending careless

beyond the etiquette of *noli me tangere*.
And yes, I know our words come close,

but they always end up shadows, or tangles
of analogue static, too worn to hear

the subtle tightening of the diaphragm
to which we all aspire. So, come here,

prove me wrong, please. Show me
your *Dasein*. I'll try to show you mine.

Epistle

Years away   or less   you do not know this song;
the way we drink to it   the stupefaction

of our dance   this girl who makes the air
gelatinous.   Your metaphors have changed;

your gut no longer turns   with her absence.
And no   our melodies are no more wedded

to the Phrygian   than are our hands content
kept clean of transgression.   Beyond this revelry

–   these riffs   that seem to hold the sun   in solstice –
I   at least   am hopeless.   Beware the academics

who have read of us   and   might try to piece together
our revival   you'll find no masterworks

amongst our debris   this is not Pompeii
nor Ercolano   there are no signs of our times.

Troia Nova

*Let us, by a flight of imagination, suppose that Rome is
not a human habitation but a psychical entity... an entity,
that is to say, in which nothing that has once come into
existence will have passed away and all the earlier phases
of development continue to exist alongside the latest one...*

SIGMUND FREUD, Civilisation and its Discontents

Gog and Magog hold the Thames at either end –
a soiled satin sheet
they billow and flutter like fresh-laundered linen.

The on-campus launderette on the Mile End Road
has only one load
rinsing at sixty, its owner nursing his hangover.

Somewhere near The George, the old El Paso,
Christopher Marlowe
wonders *what's in a name?* Scribbles *Romeo*.

Lowonida, Londinium, Lundenwic, Ealdwic;
from atomic Brythonic
to the braying of Hackneys on the Aldwych.

The braying of Hackneys on the Aldwych.
Stearns and Stetson
dithering and dodging a Johnson who shouts

cunt, from *cunte* from the Latin *cunnus*. Kit
has kicked
his horse and is trotting down Gropecuntlane

riding south to the bridge, galloping past
the traffic in which
our scholar with clean duds sits, staring

as the Lord Gordon's men breach the Newgate
(another Jonson
rehearsing the words to *Miserere mei, Deus!*).

The hydraulic *feorting* of the number twenty-five
pannikes the stallions,
the cavalry jangling in their spangly *maillots*.

Trinovantum, Caier Lud, Londres, Blackfreiris;
the black frères, the King's men,
the rustle of suits thrumming through Blackfriars.

The rustle of suits thrumming through Blackfriars.
Orare Ben Jonson,
cringing his way through a Tudor Shirley Temple.

At Temple: Knights Templar, Knights Hospitaller
abandon their temples;
one fleeing the Holy See, the other King Henry,

whose old namesake crosses the bridge, slumped
on his horse,
his sackcloth *slascht* by the Canterbury whips

and, hanging a left onto Watling Street,
passes Stearns
on the kerb whispering *che morte tanta n'avesse...*

as brogues and loafers and kitten-heels stutter
up King William Street
to Poultry and past our detergent loving docent

who has tired of the jam and decided to saunter
north (past a Johnson
twitching and grunting and turning his door-knob)

to turn left onto Clerkenwell Road, following
on the heels
of Adeline *née* Stephen now Virginia now Mrs

Woolf, quilted in furs and cradling a bouquet
through Little Italy
past a goldsmith by the name of Septimus.

Lan-dan, Douvrend, Luandun, Blemondisberi;
from Cromwell's front-gate
to the frost-bitten radicals, the December of '68.

The frost-bitten radicals, the December of '68,
flares and free-love
holding the library on Thornhaugh Street,

demanding access (full and free) to the library
on Malet Street
whilst Virginia scrawls (in a room of her own)

Vita… only with a change… from one sex to the other;
sets Orlando
shimmering and skimming a glaciated Thames

(that, currently, Kit (now Bill) now hitches
his pass over
and away from his own near-Deptford-death,

scrambling up the embankment and east
by Blackfreiris
and a Jonson whose fortunes have soured –

his head in his hands, once again muttering
Miserere mei, Deus –
as the crowd slow-clap his new 'un The New Inn).

Virginia can feel the neap tide coming in;
the waves
once spindrift then winter swell, now lap

and buffer, now siege. So, from her window
she sees
glass and beyond only water; a second pane

writhing against glass. Below: an umbrella,
Stearns dodging puddles,
shaking his umbrella onto Queens Square,

making his way up the stairs, scribbling
some of these poems...
their sustained power... emotional depth etcetera.

Nearby, our lauryl-scented lecturer
can hear sirens,
has seen each bus stalled and discarded

so mares, carriages, cabs and cortèges
pass by.
He has turned a corner onto Tavistock;

another bus is static, its top blown off.
Prepped,
a reporter settles himself to go live.

Llan Dian, Lindum, Lōnodinjon, Gislandune;
from Gough Square
to Angel and the deathbed of Islington.

The deathbed of Islington lies a little north
of this
gout-ridden Johnson who is locking his doors

whilst Stearns shuffles by or is chauffeured;
haggard,
hauling his suitcase, his well-thumbed Baedeker.

(And on to that bridge, to a train that will whisk
or beat
its way to Arnold's cliffs. And on to Paris,

to Lausanne, to those tears that rout their way
down
and drop as dabs of salt, as vital seasoning,

as galvanism for a vast fresh-water broth.
Stearns recalls
that the mind does not conceive anything

under the form of eternity, but
for its own essence
under the form of eternity...)

In Islington, Johnson has found his bed.
The black dog
slathers in the yard, bears his teeth and barks

as the first bomb drops near the village's end
and Langton tells
how Sam proclaimed his own impending death.

Lhwndin, Lunadin, Karelundein, Soersditch;
the bells seethe
in Bow, Blemondisberi, Old Bailey and Shoreditch.

The bells seethe in Bow, Blemondisberi, Old Bailey
and Shoreditch
as Leonard mopes around the library – the silence

now silence and neither hush nor rustle, nor silent
study. Outside,
the booms shudder as the Blitz reaches Brunswick.

At St Magnus-the-Martyr, Ben Jonson is baptising
his best piece of poetry,
now sobbing, now muttering *Libera me, Domine.*

At Golders Green, Stetson doffs his hat for Stearns.
On Hoop Lane,
Stearns notes a dark cloud rising from the flue.

In Westminster Abbey both Johnson and Jonson
weep
as the bodies of Jonson and Johnson are interred.

Gog and Magog hold the Thames at either end –
a soiled satin sheet
they billow and flutter like fresh-laundered linen.

On the Mile End Road, a student returns home
to call home-home,
scrolls to a number no longer listed as home.

Somewhere near The George, the old El Paso,
Shakespeare writes
A show of Eight Kings, the last with a glass in his hand.

NOTES

Dactylogram (Nietzsche) (21)
'Gott ist todt. Gott bleibt todt. Und wir haben ihn getödtet.'
translates as 'God is dead. God remains dead. And we have
killed him.' Cf. Nietzsche, *Die fröhliche Wissenschaft*.

Re: (26)
ἀλήθεια or *aletheia* is the Greek word for truth that Martin
Heidegger renders as 'unconcealedness'. Cf. Heidegger, *Parmenides*.

Elysium (29)
It was at the Battle of Alesia that Julius Caesar's army beat
a Gallic force led by Vercingétorix, a victory that precipitated
the conclusion of the Gallic Wars in Rome's favour. Cf.
Caesar, *Commentarii de Bello Gallico*. The métro station
Alesia is located in the 14th arrondissement of Paris.

III Works and Days (35)
The poem's title refers to Hesiod's *Works and Days*, which
tells the story of both Prometheus' theft from Zeus and of
Pandora's subsequent creation; it begins with the invocation
'Muses of Pieria, who give glory through song'.

Léman (39)
This poem takes its title from the French for Lake Geneva,
though the poem itself is located on Waterloo Bridge.

Carolina (47)
The poem is a collage of lines from songs by all the artists
mentioned. All songs quoted contain 'Carolina' in their title,
with the exception of 'Summertime' (from Gershwin's *Porgy
and Bess*), which is the state opera of South Carolina, USA.

Attesa (53)
The word *'attesa'* might be translated as 'attended'. Cf. Lucio
Fontana, *Concetto spaziale, Attesa*.

Ἐρινύες (60)

The contents of this poem are a near-verbatim collage of words and phrases from the artist Francis Bacon's notebooks.

Whoso list to hunt (62)

Cf. Thomas Wyatt's Sonnet XI (Rebholz edition), itself a version of Petrarch's Canzoniere 190. Wyatt's poem also contains the phrase '*noli me tangere*'.

Epistle (63)

The 'Phrygian' is, amongst other things, the name of an Ancient Greek musical mode (the equivalent of a musical key). Cf. Plato, *The Republic*.